I0801322

CHANGING RESIDENCE

NEW AND SELECTED POEMS

PREVIOUSLY PUBLISHED BY CORRADO PAINA

In Italian:

Di Corsa, Mapograph, 1996
Tempo Rubato, Atelier 14, 2004
Darsena Inquinata, Moderata Durant, 2005
Tra Rothko e tre finestre, Ibiskos, 2006
online by Tombolini Editore, 2015
L'alfabeto del viaggiatore, Silvia Editore, 2007
Abecedario, Paolo Nava Stampa, 2010
Largo Italia, SEF, 2018
Un brindisi alla malattia, SEF, 2022

In English:

Hoarse Legend—Mansfield Press, 2000
The Dowry of Education—Mansfield Press, 2004
College Street, Little Italy—Toronto's Renaissance Strip, Edited by Denis De Klerck and Corrado Paina, 2006
The Alphabet of the Traveler—Mansfield Press, 2006
Souls in Plain Clothes—Mansfield Press, 2008
Cinematic Taxi—Mansfield Press, 2014
Between Rothko and Three Windows—Quattro Books, 2016
A Toast to Illness—Quattro Books, 2018

CHANGING RESIDENCE

NEW AND SELECTED POEMS

CORRADO PAINA

Mansfield Press

Printed in Canada

Library and Archives Canada Cataloguing in Publication

Title: Changing residence : new and selected poems / Corrado Paina.
Other titles: Poems. Selections
Names: Paina, Corrado, 1954- author.
Identifiers: Canadiana 20210343850 | ISBN 9781771262774 (softcover)
Classification: LCC PS8581.A484 A6 2021 | DDC C811/.6—dc23

Cover Image: Deborah Verginella
Author Photo: Deborah Verginella

The publication of *Changing Residence, New and Selected Poems* has been generously supported by the Canada Council for the Arts and the Ontario Arts Council.

ONTARIO ARTS COUNCIL
CONSEIL DES ARTS DE L'ONTARIO
an Ontario government agency
un organisme du gouvernement de l'Ontario

Canada Council for the Arts
Conseil des arts du Canada

Mansfield Press Inc.
25 Mansfield Avenue, Toronto, Ontario, Canada M6J 2A9
Publisher: Denis De Klerck
www.mansfieldpress.net

to Luciano Iacobelli,
cor cordis, heart and art

PREFACE

This is only the second time, in twenty-three years as a publisher, that I have written a preface in one of the books that I published. The first time wasn't *for* Corrado Paina, it was *with* him, in a preface for *College Street/Little Italy: Toronto's Renaissance Strip*. That book, published in 2004, documented the street and the communities who populated it from the earliest days in Toronto. The two of us worked on it together and it went on to win a City of Toronto Book Award. This was the neighbourhood we both called home and, truthfully, we secretly thought of ourselves as part of the renaissance referred to in the title and we wanted to document it somehow.

We met in the mid 1990s when College St. was undergoing the rapid transformation that we thought of as a renaissance. It had been a street of mom-and-pop retail and smoke-filled sports bars for working class men. One of these was Bar Italia—a simple place to drink espresso and play pool, or boccette, at least until Eugene Barone bought the business and began serving an inventive menu of sandwiches, salads, thoughtfully chosen wines, and grappa. The clientele changed almost overnight. It was one of the few places on the street that women felt welcome, and it was quickly adopted by the arts community.

In 1995 I was hired by Bar Italia to be the General Manager of the new, two-storey expansion being built next door. This is where I met Corrado and discovered we shared a common interest in poetry. Corrado wrote about Canada, but in Italian, and the language barrier meant he had few readers. I was a voracious reader, especially of poetry, so I was naturally curious about his work, though I didn't speak Italian.

Eventually Corrado had some of his poetry translated and shared it. I immediately saw it was different from the poetry I was reading from English Canada. The tone was heart-on-the-sleeve passionate—something Canadians, including me, are generally too polite to show. The poetry was also angry and political and filled with sharp observations of the multicultural social life of Toronto. There was a street-level awareness that can only come from a recent immigrant who has had to adjust to a new country and the nuances of a new language. He was also alive to the language of the Italian Canadian community which developed among the immigrants who arrived here in the 1950s and 60s. Known as 'Italese,' it is a conflation of English and Italian that grew organically in Canadian soil. Growing up in Milan, Corrado had no reason to speak Italese but it's a goldmine worth exploring for a poet concerned with how language is transformed over time.

Joseph Brodsky, a great poet of exile, once observed that "geography blended with time equals destiny." Corrado moved from Italy to Canada at a time when the Italian Canadian community was already well established. His work—his destiny if you like—is to always stand a little outside of the Canadian mainstream and a little outside the Italian Canadian community he is now a part of.

This is what intrigued me when I first read his work. Writers who are Canadian born and bred don't write like this. And the Canadian writers with a strong connection to a home country also don't write like this. The former are too far removed from the immigrant experience to write about it accurately, and the latter often reflect on the country of their birth nostalgically. Paina doesn't do this. He looks back only to understand the present. He writes about what's in front of him, which can sometimes be painful, and not what is behind him, beyond change.

My own destiny was certainly bound to the time and place that Corrado and I first met. By 1996, the new Bar Italia opened and was instantly and massively popular. It provided a home for an incredibly diverse group of cultural initiatives that would eventually have great success. Knopf Canada launched their inaugural "New Face of Fiction" series there and introduced the world to Yann Martel, Ann Marie Macdonald, Gail Anderson Dargatz and Dionne Brand, a remarkable group of first-time novelists. We also hosted countless book launches for a wide variety of Canadian publishers. The Hot Docs Film Festival was still in its infancy, and we hosted their press conferences and provided a venue to show films before they had a home of their own. Outpost magazine and Toro magazine regularly had editorial meetings at the bar as they got their award-winning projects off the ground; the designer Bruce Mau had a regular table; and Bruce Macdonald was making films down the street. I could name-drop for a couple of more pages, but you get the point: the place was generally crawling with writers, actors, painters, architects, designers, musicians, and filmmakers. New bars and restaurants were soon opening all along College Street, and they also tended to attract an arts crowd.

It was in this hothouse atmosphere that Corrado and I were discussing his work one day, and his inability to publish, and, on a whim, in a fit of madness, because everyone else seemed to have an interesting project on the go, I said I would publish him if no one else would. In an unconscious imitation of Knopf's New Face of Fiction, I also invited Diana Fitzgerald Bryden, Ann Shin, and Margaret Christakos to be part of the inaugural Mansfield Press list. It was everyone's first book except for Margaret, who was already an established writer. The books launched in 2000 and I'm happy to say all four of them went on to be award-winning writers.

W.H. Auden famously said that "poetry makes nothing happen," but that hasn't been my experience. For the last 23 years poetry has been a cause with unforeseen effects in my life. For one thing, creating Mansfield Press completely changed how I make my living, while simultaneously draining my bank account and delaying my retirement indefinitely. I should have seen that one coming. But it also allowed me to join a conversation with talented, passionate writers who normally wouldn't give me the time of day as a restaurant worker. And for that I can thank, and, depending on the day, blame, Corrado Paina.

Twenty-three years after this whole adventure began it seems appropriate to look back and gather some material from the books we have done together. *Changing Residence* documents the conflicts and resolutions of a restless writer who has spent a lifetime traveling the world to document what he finds there. Raised in Italy, with its old-world perspective, and settled in Canada amid the babel of its grand multicultural experiment, Paina's poetry, over the course of many books, has been an evolutionary and revolutionary response to the accident of birth that separates humans from each other and the cultural bonds we forge to bridge that separation. Michael Redhill has called Paina's work "a celebration of homelands old and new," but it is also a passionate social critique of the very concept of a 'homeland.' *Changing Residence* gathers in one place, the trajectory of an artist who has remained curious, committed, and engaged with whatever 'home' he happens to land in.

Denis De Klerck
October, 2022

HOARSE LEGEND

(2000)

HONEST ED'S AND THE TEMPLES OF SWEAT (1987)

to Deborah

CANARY WHARF

another day unfolds
to repeat the language
of an advanced lineage

dominant races with confused grimaces
in the shadows of Charlottetown
in the variety stores of Meech Lake

the damp streetcars don't provide shelter
or work   on a journey backwards
zealous porters escort to Limbo

we leave theatres under the bridges
we leave Cubans in exile that
scatter notes like croissants

look

waning is the drunkenness of the aboriginals
now reclined, crucified from dizziness

the stench of chamber pots floods Queen Street
in that corner where the streetcar observes silently

eloquent rows of immigrants' children
that want to enter

Pizza!
fast janissaries challenge heavy artillery
for a delivery
look

the times of flags are not over
upon the banner slides the ethnic resin
men and women
in uniform
awaken a drunk

THEY ARE NOT ADMITTED INTO THE LAND OF LAKES THOSE EMBRACING THEIR OWN SHADOW drowned in a puddle of vomit the sidewalk drenched read

here in the charter of rights
there is no room for
infibulations, turbans, polygamy, sexual violence,
purges, smokers, only tomato in de bekiarda

in the world of errant farmers
they don't plant homosexuality
they till the earth

and they forgive only the animals

the Chinese get on the streetcar
older than the temples of sweat
they don't ask for directions

or buy citizenships

towards the Communist temple
the Long Realty March
brings new invasions

barbarians

the mortgages rebound of the walls of the Reichmans
the fate of the
umane genti is shattered

I return home inebriated from a wedding of the masses

respect ancestries
and blood

no more entwining   no lovers' quarrels
too many envelopes to count
who will show the sheets stained with blood...

on the balcony the geraniums shimmer
moist with musk
the old men watch blindly

dear mother
they have put hounds in front of the gates
to defend villas, Palladio
lucky for him! is dead,
here they are all presidents, mother
the houses have more columns than the Parthenon
they erected a long wall that surrounds their homes
perhaps it is better like this

they have the cars of the Italian rich
but they make more noise

they have children that are proud of their Italian origin
when they beat up a transvestite

mother we are in an Italy that is not of the north
nor of the center nor of the south
it isn't shaped like a boot
perhaps a patent leather shoe

mother I could tell you many things
but I must say goodbye

p.s. mother dear mother
                u' zappatore
                died
                yesterday
                of cirrhosis of the liver
                the organ wounded
                by wartime echoes of must

GARBAGE FOR ALL SEASONS

I always felt like a citizen of the world until
I walked the streets of Toronto
the global village spreads the hundred odors of a thousand
foods cooked and not, according to custom
and the urban waste of a thousand races
each with its own little
green bag to forget
pluriracial factories of rheum sweat shit
multiculturalism for a thousand multidisposals
italojamaican indochinese
blackwhites yellowreds
canada all-inclusive+separatism and a trip to cuba
warm warmth violent cyclothymic
dio! come sa di sale lo pane altrui

OPEN COLLEGE

the bars of College street are opening
open Brooklyn
you of granita
and of espressos
tables on the sidewalks and children of immigratory waves

the Chinese State knocks noisily
"we will stop them on the waterline!"
from pool halls upstairs
appear young portuguese

night falls with a group of vietnamese
knifing each other
("sons of war" they say)
at night a gang of vigilantes
clean-shaven italoportojapokrainian
maybe chase a car thief

the yell in english
poly, multi thugs

open College

they could close off the area
like in Rome
and put tables
in the streets!
the summer is different on College
and the distant sirens
belong
to the city
on College bells are ringing
on College firetrucks are a civic event
on College they know you

on College there is a vagrant
that everyone knows
and that goes back and forth
along College
the pantograph of a streetcar
tears through the viscera of the sky
hunks of watermelon
bits of pistachio ice cream
scraps of tomato
and threads of parmesan and pecorino
rain
upon the tables of College

ITALIAN SATURDAY

the area awakens to the sound
of AlfaRomeo and Cherokees
"It's Saturday"
a spring Saturday
we must air out the garages
"wake up Nina and put on your best dress!"
Tony will buy cannoli
while nonno hoes the bekiarda
to plant flowers and not tomatoes
like they taught him
(in adult education)

here in the Petawawa of the rich
of the less rich and of the neveragain poor
the sun shines italian

it's nice to see the cotrarelli
playing be-se-ból
in the streets
and the old men sitting on the steps near
the neoclassic garage

it's warm and the linen clothes are lying
on the bed still fragrant
double-breasted suits and flowered shirts from
florida

the mothers and the nonnas are preparing cannelloni
the wine stirs in the cellars
waiting for relatives   friends
how nice it is to walk along the empty streets of
Woodbridge

knowing each other
after years in the neighborhood
there are no cafes
there are no shops
the pools still dirty
the trees so young

there is shade only
near the neoclassic garages
there are no barbers
pharmacists
and the priest...

... it is an italian sun
that beats down on Woodbridge
flowered Woodbridge
one day they will put benches
for the old men
confined in their maximum security bekiardas

THE TRANSLATED MESSAGES DON'T ARRIVE

not the thunderous cries of the last orator
nor the double-face flyers

we are ashamed of our ignorance
italia what is left of us? in us?

we have no clothing to wash in Don Mills and our
empire survives in the busts of il Duce
we will build other ghettos for our children and
the other races to come

after us Ceramicaland
Woodbridge on the lake
Morgheggioville...
here where the highways
lead to the italian enclave
the messages brought by the last orator
don't arrive

"We have built it all and now we own it..."
in the summer old men resemble street signs
in the still Italian corridors

PARADISE OF CITIZENSHIP

I am horny for the community's triumph
I inhale global villages
sub tegmine fagi
I titillate multicultural clitorises

Expo
god
if you are in your heaven
if you don't have a colour
a language
a tribal mask
an Alinari photo
show me the paradise of shitizenship

I don't want to die here
because my pride of fatherland
is boundless
insatiable like my appetite
not mediterranean but prehistoric
I'm the one who wants to be hyphenated
when he makes love   at least
I'm Rossi's coffee pot, towered, babelic
I'm an angel in underwear by Chia
and I'm an angel in brocade by Beato Angelico
I'm as desolate as a factory by Sironi
I'm the premature brother of Rocco
the brick and the pick of the Wall
I'm confined for the short time of a life
I'm a chameleon of ethnicity
but not a merchant
I'm the helmsman who falls asleep

Expo
god
unveil to me the paradise of shitizenship

HONEST ED'S AND THE TEMPLES OF SWEAT

didn't you see them?   the races
sucking their teeth
spitting on subway platforms
throwing a hundred pounds of meat on the barbecue
buying tons of sugar
for fear of war
going into big stores
bait of voracious sects

dreaming of wardrobes with mirrored doors
buying bread and bread
stowing supermarket bags in the trunks of
american cars
buying gold and gold

sleeping in immigration offices
queued to go to unknown factories
in the suburbs of your sight
unloaded by a bus
on a Sunday

DISCOUNTS
on leg of lamb
in line at the food-banks
in lines faint, drowsy, feverish

can't you see the fear of poverty
the steps of a second life
slippery from sweat?

sleeping little and always being sleepy
the brain wearied
from different languages

there are weddings
already marked by the violence of broken dreams
you so young
will lose your ethnic shape

will become fat and pakistani
you a varicose portuguese

your children will play be-se-ból
the turkish grandmother will watch football games on
television

you will build a fence around
your italian meatball
and put a sign on it
"PLEASE DON'T REMIND ME OF THE PAST"

THE MURDER OF BOSSI

you looked at me with vacuous eyes
when I spoke of Gramsci
you asked me
if this italy was a civilized country

you will find three lines at customs
one for the european community
one for the rest of the world
and one for i terroni

fate la nanna coscine di pollo
sweet italocanadian spy
mentre la nonna cucina il cavallo
from the south to the north in less than a month
sotto il ponte di Baracca
you left to kill Bossi
c'é Pierin che fa la cacca
you are not afraid of hills and streams

Baggio, Rozzano, Quarto Oggiaro
it isn't easy
to recognize the old ghettos
from the new... and Giambellino

children of Europe
that do not run
faster than Miglio

darknesses distant and heavy
Bari or Toronto
the young play
and copulate
kneeling before the Samnites

the fog has covered the countryside
nature is on all fours
sodomized it whispers
"at your disposal"

the farmers still talk to the animals
the races, colours speak of values
"*more justice is needed*"

ex-nations ask for money
from happy states
the fog asks for kickbacks
blood is seen and not seen

you imagine that the countryside was here
but do you see it?

in the shadow of the monument to the injured worker
artists ambulate
they talk about everything

of cousins that arrived empty-handed
of funerals that cost too much
of italians that have abandoned their homes

of basamenti to rebuild
of whorish daughters
of property tax

you have left to kill Bossi
without knowing who Gramsci is
you don't know what it means to rest
in the shade of a Party

weakened by sweet domestic violence
you have left without permission
in the name of honour
indifferent to the banners
of Petawawa
to the calls of the sirens
emerging from the oceans of Woodbridge
sickened by the plankton
of malls

I wish for you the bench of infinity

CINEMATIC TAXI

a taxi of an ex-colonel of the
afghan army or a
somali refugee
or perhaps of a milanese survivor
travels the streets without time
and without memory

Toronto
the streets are empty even when
there are people

avenues
lashed by wind
journeys of solitary titans

it's not a city for lovers   Toronto
the streets are long and wide
the buildings severe
the complicitous doorways are in Milan

you too little girl torn away
by ethnic cleansing
for your personal hygiene
toast with a jamaican taxi driver
just stopped by the police

toast for shitizenship
wanted
desired
fornicated
defecated
and then swallowed again

taxi driver
let's sing the national anthem
to the sound of the meter

MULTICULTURAL CHRISTMAS

the buildings in Comasina echo
from petit bourgeois christmases
to the roots of condominiums
kinetic junkies

in the spirals of housing projects
jamaican progeny
develop in darkness

italians clean fish
cries of a hundred babies
and neighborhoods in a frenzy

exhalations of incense
vomiting of curry and parked taxis
faint but strong-willed
a song makes its way
to my room

amore love amor
we are all immigrants
you are not excluded either
diaphanous jew
alone and without ideology
persecuted for a hundred years by the Bolsheviks

you will be there too cuban engineer
bonus in a tourist package
(walking one day with a flag)
toward the Skydome

no one is absent from the roll-call of races,
of origins, of creed
it is the christmas of the Charter of Rights

disloyal Lolita toast to your
arrogance
fondled by suburban DJ's

you too are set in jewelry

... you too radiant princess
without jewels and without a land
infatuated with the last multicultural hybrid

and you that once
were a whore of the lebanese
and perhaps could confer upon yourself the title

of pearl of the West

today you have a son and a husband
from the third world
a Harvard graduate
a polyglot son

only because there are no more revolutions
you do not have to spend winters
in the bosom of your mother
you
will return
like all the thousands
the hundreds of thousands
of chinese, latin american,
from ex-nations
from ex-states

maybe there will no longer be gigantic waves
inevitably
pulled by the undertow
onto these beaches

it is a snowstorm that is coming
we will learn
to show our most beautiful colours
multi-coloured balls
for the christmas tree

EBOLI

to Deborah

awakened from the American dream
when on the prairies
public housing is being erected
stifling the view

Rome and Kensington market
burn
but no one knows

hosts of seagulls
fly on the rotten plain
distant smells shatter
against the doors of neoclassic garages

the air-conditioners are useless
against the fumes
of Caribana

hypothesizing in the streets
the tanks of Pinochet
and of Krushev
are parked at the borders

portuguese italians somalis palestinians

the ethnics

work in agencies for cleansing

algid garbage mutates
like a stone smoothed
and inevitably crushed
by the undertow

the windows
of Yonge Street shatter
beneath the pressure of exuberant hydrants
clitorises are mutilated
death penalties in parking lots
t-shirts soaked with beer

in front of monotonous televisions
hyperventilated populations
watch from porches
mute and nostalgic

generations without remote control
sweat profusely
at the shows
of democracy

filthy!
where Socrates' pædophilia is punished
by millennia
hemlock and castor oil
for the ghosts of High Park

mixed couples
pornoanglophone triangles
respectful and calvinistic families
they don't leave a tip
on the tables
of the latest italian restaurant

Toronto
I want to smoke a cigarette
I want to become a cigarette
the smoke for a hundred thousand allergy sufferers
I am the Masaniello of the smoking section
I want to fly onto plates of eggplant and zucchini

to mix myself into the fierce curries
to roll myself in a fajita
like boric acid fumarole to stir rice and chicken
to ride the draft of an air conditioner
to camouflage myself in the hundred year old dust of
carpeting

to trans-humanize with the pots in Chinatown
like a poisonous gust of wind to stiffen the backs
of a thousand baby-kissing politicians
I would be the bad breath of repentant DJ's
the chloroses of the running multitudes
the fetid and caustic membrane
of shining skyscrapers

fly with me
toward the last recesses of a health conscious democracy
permeate the pulmonary basements
of this city that doesn't know how to scream
like a Harpy
I would like to sprinkle amber
on the beaches
of our solitude

AFTERNOON UNKNOWNS

TRIANGLE

I let my right hand adventure
before falling asleep on my side
with a last palpation
on the rotundity of her belly

I heard nothing
maybe the bubbling of a concealed spring
I put a finger in her lips
and closed my eyes

she clung to me
thigh on femur
hand playing
with penis

a gold doubloon
appearing and disappearing through
the crest of the water
over a cliff
until the palm
shaded it

we snoozed until the wind woke us up

maybe we should close the window
she whispered indolent
and unveil our treasure

of warmth
woven of smell
breath and
sighs

raise the curtain of
sheets and quilts
locked in this theatre
you are the chosen one

the harbour
of my shoulders
shelters the coldness of
your chin
your
abandoned ship

I stood up and
I almost pushed her back
wrapped up
in our wings

weighed down by honey
and arrogance
pale
in an escape from the sun

I have closed the window
and the wind whimpers
his limb cut off

catch the breast soon feeding two mouths
nipples like norman towers
spread above two peaks
in the Scopello bay

I entered a cave

crowded by bats
before my penis was attacked by
a thousand drones

we kicked sheets and quilts
and pillows
so that our screams were not
suffocated

and
we praised the lord
or was it
the Butterfly's humming choir

you came three or two moments
before me and your orgasm
has been confirmed
by mine

I'm dripping –
and she disappears
in the washroom
that was never outdoors

but the sound of the wounded wind
is whispering in my ear that
she is climbing the hill
to the latrine

inside there's a candle and
a man with a kilt
who lifts her with the
frantic arms of the patriot and screws her

cradling my thoughts
on the pillow
I fall asleep

cold screams
of hookers
crying from nostalgia

bottles shattered against
my walls
needles piercing the wallpaper

and our souls
separated by heaven
for a while
the long while of the heat

BOOKS

to Marco Giomini

guards waiting at the door
and they are all beautiful
like cuirassiers
oh the books!

the books that I had read
sucked
abandoned

the rejected books
licked
damp
tumid

introverted titles
behind a veil
of mourning

oh the books!

with cavities
the liver swollen
the colic
the anxiety crisis
the irregular heart beat

spread your legs encyclopædia of the theatre,
of philosophy,
... marsilio was not born in marseille
gadamer's house doesn't shelter me

calvino's books are flying
i will catch them

oh the books
that cry!
i can't stand them
i throw a stone at them
they will yelp

ssss don't turn on the light
they have cat's eyes
this tome is rubbing
its thick and clean hair

dance salome's dance for me
beautiful bayadere
on the plate a bleeding book

you whisper to me to not trust
those golden letters
are your bracelets
tinkling in the abattoir

or is it the cracking glue?

i
a written book
in a book
conceived in 1954

was it a good year for books?
the god of Roserio
and which others?
i have just read it
and all the others are in the incubator
pages stuck with sperm
pages disfigured by the blade

pages that open themselves
when you titillate the morocco
gushing pages
hidden by haughty gates
pages
        pages of
                        pages of books
oh the books!

DEATH

doctors sacked souls and bodies
then what remained of us
went back to life

cheerful you ran toward me
contradicting death
as the poet wrote

you gave me a prescription of
morphine
and i was in the hotel
again and again

it's not that i have
always been living like that
but the shapes of luck
won't be familiar to you

i'm here looking at
the city of pestilence
making your wings
fly higher
beyond frames
windows and houses
dogs and gods
men and leaves

we exchange nudities
exploring the labyrinth
of unknown walls
of afternoon unknowns

falling asleep
to forget that

once we were close
so close
to the sun
swimming arrogantly
through the wave of its rays.

GEOMETRY

to ilario, andrea and to the lari

they were two straight lines
respectively on a
lambretta and on a vespa

they met at the rotunda
of sesto
to become a point

to cover the segment
of the tangential of
cinisello

mario of bar sport
hid his fireflies
in a box of matches

in a corn field
under a big metal ear
they opened the box

they left when
the night
might also be day

the fireflies turn on and
off
until death

the point
collapsed
dismembered into two tangents

divergent
respectively on a
lambretta and on a vespa

THE DOWRY OF EDUCATION

(2004)

POEMLESS BUS

there are buses without poems
perhaps because the passenger
is still dozing
there are buses without sounds
perhaps because there's too much thinking
not centric but
peripheral thought, that of
mad monads created
by the big bang of imploded mortgages
the black hole of a repetitive job
the marks of race
and so we all go
mute on a poemless, readerless, storytellerless bus
waiting for the stop where the adolescents
will bring their sparrow cries
of school homework and theoretical sex

SCREENING THE FLOOD

I am awake! I am listening!
my ear pressed at the wall of my skin
I know there are rivers
I can hear their foaming roar
the fragile rafts of life crashing
against debris of malignant fractions
and corpses floating
paying the price for their uprising

my ear can listen to the dark
my eyes can screen the greediness of
crowded pipelines or the abandoned carwash
in my intestine

pain is burning thorns in my
temples
racing on free highways

and fear
fear that everything will stop
and I will be the scab the lonely scab
in front of the large gate to death

TORONTO

to Nelda and Sergio

I have been at times negligent
my eyes crawling with ingratitude
there were affairs with towns and remote cities
small squalid business

I go back sometimes to old love stories
just to hurt myself
I have been disloyal
lured into quick and forgettable infidelities
with bridges
rivers and churches

we lit a cigarette for each other
we had doorway sex
hiding from art and design
I thought they were looking for me

I invented forefathers and stepfathers
floating in a basket over the stream of
nostalgia

I am coming back to tell you
that my name is nobody
your only eye still raptured
and innocent

WATERMELON

Listen to the advice of the silent monolith. Inside there are sugary creatures. Screaming geysers of liquid glucose. Seed of blood sausages, viscera well laid out. You have killed its soul with a vulgar deed, cutting its extremities to violate its peace. You will be punished by a big wave that will swallow your screams. Listen when you knock on its walnut door to an apartment left by the tenants, and when lingering on the steps, imagine the children running. You will think you hear the happy shouts of games. This reconciled Red Sea is like a flag over a body. Inside the red planet there are hidden and loquacious springs where one can quench his thirst. Where one can bathe. Inside there is emptiness, like a box enveloped in precious tapestries, there is tepid light water, there's the sleep of the infant and the well's smell of its flower breath.

IN AN OLD CANADIAN TRUNK

to Luca

there are old newspapers with today's titles
and a book of outdoor life
enveloped in dust and dark
a postcard of a giftless english christmas
sprinkled with polluted carols
and a wooden goose
which seems turned into
a pillar of salt by boredom
the open wings stalled
over the sameness
there is a small accordion
whose music ended after the
hundredth beer
a doll, there's always a doll
whose hands have scars
whose lips are covered by the great snow
of 1889
a pair of gloves for hands lost in
ivory hymnals
and a journal of accounts
where you added wrinkles
deducting days
the smell
only the smell is the same
of any old trunk hiding the
horror of all who lose their eyes
in the endless quest
along the endless mile

PASSPORT SIZE PHOTOGRAPH

The photograph on my passport is more extraneous to me than my image in the mirror, more unpredictable than advice, more refractory than Ungaretti's stone of San Michele, more irreversible than a used match, more unsolvable than the white sheet. I am not talking about the future that has already gone. In the photograph is a me who was and is not anymore—therefore I am no longer the person who appears with a part of my already thin hair cut off by the shortsighted scissors of the photographer. It's not me because I have never been. That face belongs to other professions, other stories, other lives in other galaxies. The photographer should think, before taking pictures, about the responsibilities of his profession. To take a deontologically correct picture, the photographer should ask for a criminal record, an anamnesis and a 25/30 line max. , small biography. And, if it is possible, a series of photographs taken previously by less scrupulous colleagues of his. You are laughing at a pathetic face that cannot be mine, imagine it could be yours . . . we are laughing at a person's face that does not exist . . . perhaps it is dead.

EUPHEMISM

to Alberto Casiraghy

Sunflowers, withered sunflowers. Dead. It is not usual. They are not ordinary flowers. They bend like American willows with big beehive faces—the stems still erect, like rusty drills and then the broken neck. Did you leave them on purpose? I mean there, on the table, to say that we have fought and we are approaching our withering, our wrinkling. They heavily occupy a good part of the table in that jaundiced pot. One cannot but notice them. Nobody says a word. Perhaps you didn't even see them because I am the only one for you. I should be flattered but what I feel is just a pure sensation of decadence joined to a bad odour. To get rid of it I should smell the water of the sunflowers. Maybe you have left them there just as you didn't make the bed, as you didn't flush the toilet, as I didn't shave or shower. We are the only ones. Imagine if we bent our heads as though our necks could not hold the weight of thinking about decadence and death. Imagine if we were in the yellowish pot and the sunflowers were sitting at the table wondering whether to throw us away. I remember only one literary reference about sunflowers and it is Rimbaud pissing in front of them. I like the pissing thing. It is majestic. But I won't talk about it to you because it is not the day. It's a Sunday, a weekend day, a holiday with death.

IN A GLASS BOX

to Tom Thompson

once the old palette lies
under a sky of glass
it cannot tell us much
the choice remains mysterious
the colours drowned in a muddy whirlpool
all of them
like a collective suicide in a river
in the end the palette is a corpse
it is difficult to believe that the blood
the bark of the birch tree
the smiling face of the snow
the lingering leaf undecided
between the passion of the wind and the
affection of the stream
were all in it
in the end what remains of us
lies faded at the bottom of the river

THE POET WAS WRONG

to Max Arrigoni

The poet was wrong.
With death in thousands
the thoughts crammed
multiplied in postcards of architecture
and landscapes
drowned in fiery water.

The poet was wrong.
Separation unplugged memory
eroding monuments carried away
through streams of debris.

The poet was wrong.
Books shook up in fire
and children queued
in assembly lines
eyes, games,
teeth and embraces
ripped off.

The poet was wrong.
Burning pyre of remembrances
to tear the darkness with learning
burning the wings of childhood
to protect the purity of ourselves.

The poet is wrong.

BLUE CAKE OF DREAMS

to Andrea

Sleep little treasure
your snowy blankets
have the consistent passion
of the wave
the very eternity of the landslide

sleep until morning
tomorrow your blue birthday cake
will remind you
of the obtuseness of your weight
and the coquetry of the sky

for you can't know the ordeal

green is your colour
of choice or brown for
we
crawling like ants
on the earthly skull
are condemned to watch
the forbidden blue
scarred by the crown of flowers
and tired arrows of grass

you are kicking walls of air
sleep castaway
from the titans' land
resume your travel
stowaway of life

you will be taught
the language of cannibals

someone will inform you
that you are a dormant volcano
that the cicadas' song
dies in the fall

how cruel
teaching is
I beg for your forgiveness
while kissing the soles
of your sleepless little feet

WE CALL YOU ROSE PETAL

to Andrea

the playground has been erased
my child is stirring the sand
like a gentle hurricane

there are only basketball players
and dope smokers
postdamer platz hangers
hidden in the corners
of the concrete entrances
doors of wind and dope
first sex first aid
we are alone
Andrea and I
where are the other children?

she pulls from the sand
a chocolate cake
where the dog was spinning
seagulls fight for leftover *masa*
and pasta
sparrows and pigeons
learn about hierarchy

where are the other children?
for me the sand is the hand of the sea
for you it is the whole universe

our memories don't collide
my memories don't enlighten you
yours are beyond the clouds
the bridge of the milky way
is inaccessible to me

I love you with my smallness
you are life for an illness
your solitude is mine
mine the sins mine the guilt
emerging from your sand
which you stir like a gentle hurricane

TONIGHT I AM THE STATE

to Massino Ma Cho Cozzi, Erio D'angelo, Sergio Sgaramella

La maldita circunstancia del agua por todas partes
Virgilio Piñera

this queue is drawing my blood
like the mosquito of the dawn
this rum is discolouring desire
only the cheek of the child is paler than this milk
even today this line springs from promises
and ends up with history

I have learnt to entertain myself with useless questions
is the queue longer than the waiting?
is the waiting longer than the queue?
is hope begotten by the fight or the fight begotten by hope?
is it better to be in good health or to be free?
the faces of the missing
of those who have attempted the ocean
are not painted on the walls

José Antonio Ernesto Camilito
in my sole dream
there is a gate to heaven
though it could be hell
without a queue
without libreta
if you were not here I'd feel lonelier
than the crab in the middle of the road
his claws lifted against the indifferent tire

the fear that all our dead
our heroes
if they were alive
would tell us to resist

just like when I hit your chest
don't come before me

hold on! hold on!
think about him!

think about the Lider Maximo
against the Americans

but if I think about him
I'll come too soon

then think about the dead!
our dead
remember Frank Pais remember Abel Santamaria
remember Camilo Cienfuegos
remember Ché
Hatuey
José Martí

imagine the gods waking up inside the palms
and beating along the drum tree
blood leaks in tears scenting History

think about the slaughter of the pigs
about the gold which ran out
leaving a bitter taste
think about the breath of gall sweetened by
the tobacco leaf

about the armoured train blowing up in anger

let's root love
because the heat glues us for hours

and we unglue with free trajectories
you are the cuntpiercing cormorant
I am the peniscatcher falcon
while screams with hooks and beaks
resound in this room
shreds colouring the walls
into a large magna square
where we fly over you
asshole smeller
then I descend on a branch
and I dance waiting to fall asleep
waiting for the bat's singing

(ready or not, here I come . . .)
a life under embargo
is like a fly zipped forever
a sea that carries only to the coast
a plane which only lands and never leaves

we who were born with the embargo
cannot distinguish the outside from the inside
it is a voice from birth
growing despite the queue the libreta
the dead the gods
despite your love for me
the heat and the mosquitoes
it is the slap of the wave whipping itself

ready or not
here I come

the malnourished dancers dismantle the set of Giselle
and they go to the Tropicana and dance with the tourists
lured by the illusion the prince dances to death
the slave wins the slaver
hugging the tourist
all this movement makes me hungry

History will absolve me
nothing more boring
than Cristianos y Moros
it is like watching an action movie
at Cubavision
where heroes are cane cutters
peasants are philosophers of the local cell
and heroes never shut up

rice and beans
at Radiorebelde the uncommitted rotten youth
take drugs in Colombia
whore out in Puerto Rico

dignity in black and white
the country sits at the table
Cristianos y Moros
the balsero approaches the coral customs

despacio
the warrior
who left children and conflicts
who headed to the hundred fires
was terminated by the leprosy
he wanted to cure
he lays on a pallet portrayed by the local mantegna

lost battles became miracles
his evangelic writings
were traded and altered into apocrypha

now his face is impressed
on a thousand shrouds
his body buried somewhere
and so many are waiting for his return

the breeding of Varadero
like each imperial morning
the crooked and wrinkled laborers
were waiting for Monsieur Dupont
who was late
they spat on the dry land

I am hanging around with a little bit of money
among breeding bulls and cows to be bred
I am waiting for the results of the blood test
I must wait for a month at least
I'll call up the doctor once I'm at home

I have left Alvadys with unavoidable doubts
you almost engineer without ruler
without pads

Heiida you are hiding your sole condom
in your bra
you'll keep it alive like an old Chevy
you'll turn it out and you'll turn it in

you are not my Friday
you told me that after three days
I would not remember your face

I am your State
tonight I am your Lider Maximo

I kidnapped you
farm animal
grown in the dark

you write me that you got married and you have a child
grown in the dark
the son of *periodo especial*

you are so distant so discoloured
that your letters seem epigraphs

sleep old pontiac sleep my esposa
I loved you more than any woman
like a woman you had colours and sounds

we were together
in the countryside on the mountain at the seaside
in Pinar in Havana in Santa Clara
in Camaguey
in Varadero
you are so counterrevolutionary that
you loved and have begotten children without ideologies

sucio is the sea, filthy, rotten
despite a blue smile
this water wicked with attrition
coitus
coral phalluses
humorous jelly fishes
mobile foams
tears of rum
horizons of concrete

this sea to wear
like an invisible cloak
fills up buddies and pals
vaginas assholes mouths
rubs the eyes of the nation
discolouring the island

burns like Deianira's tunic
like the flame of Hatuey
with the fire that the pyre cannot extinguish
the pain of farewell

tonight I am the State
that night my senses were jamming
the bed sheet restlessly fluctuating
smell of milk
pouring from her armpits
from her lavic breast

then her curls sprouted from
the white ploughed pillow
thin and shining waves
blown by a timid moon

her eyelids were gates for the bull
her lips were the quicksand of forgiveness
but her hands
were not curious
not voracious

tonight I am the State
Cristianos y Moros
I am bartering an old drunken boat
and American twins
for your shining sprouts

we bite our breath in the silence

it was me it was you
sea animals in the sunset
you emerging from the silent sky-struck sea

your belly still beating in a far country

walk, keep walking
wait
wait and walk

the breathing of the exhausted engine
has stopped
walk until the victory
walk to Havana

wait for the truck loading
the doctors the peasants the workers
walk to the horizon
to the unattainable victory
to the imperial customs

you were born like the god inside a palm
and inside a palm you have grown up
spying on men and animals

you have waited for the barbarians
the counter-revolutionaries

vigia
you pretended to be asleep in a barrack
emasculated by playa Giron and Escambray
you had screened the horizon of asphalt

in your dream you are surrounded by the worms of Mariel
by balseros by jineteras

you are smiling
because you are holding a flaming sword
angel of an exhausted god

Sierra
you've asked for help from everybody
and you've helped everybody
your love has been defended
and profaned
by men in different uniforms

regular irregular soldiers
conquistadores barbudos
cristianos y moros
their wishes burn out
their bodies punished by dreams and clouds

your herbs have cured asthma
your eyes have diagnosed the fevers
your arms have dug the graves of the dead

you've undone the canvas
and concede yourself to no one

S.S.Granma
we are still on our journey
and aren't you tired
of all these weary warriors?
Roland has sold his Durendal

the poet tunes his lyre
he is not singing of the repentance
he sings of the rejected counter-revolution
the sacrifice of life

even today
there's no land on the horizon
the poet cannot see
he is counting the wrinkles of silence
(I am still alive May 18)

Cuba
in charge of universal responsibility
I in a little field
pushing the ploughshare
what a life is life
when the moon on the clear sea

round and fat
pale and whimsical
fantasizes
and begs standing at the corner of a cloud
and then she goes and rests
deaf to my pains

I am lonely in the island of poverty and nature
ahi! the trumpet of the sun is pushing
breakfast time and cigars
one two three
I am in charge of universal responsibility

you bartered the Hippocratic oath
for a box of ammunition

your motorbike blocked by the
Periodo Especial

you could drive for nations and continents
death has dueled with you
perhaps you thought you could win
and for your arrogance she
has cut off your hands

Nuestra America
to me the Indies are a few miles away
between the sea and the dream

I know that our dead
will not approve
searching like sentinels the sea customs
the arrival of the felucca and of the airplane
greeting the foreign delegation that brings
precious spices and monsters

the country moans and bleeds with
interrupted orgasms
you hug me and like hummingbirds
we take the pleasure of limited ellipsis
if you were not here
with me I'd forget
health
education
the country and the Sierra

because Cuba is an island
island of zafra
of absolution of libreta and querida presencia

but the sea
scented with freedom and flight
is a concrete trunk
it is a hero and a betrayer
it is alive and cemeterial

Nuevitas
my house is not here
not here where the pale beaches
blind the tourist with beauty
and the palms are confessionals of the sun god

my house is where love
is scented by the jewels of Yemayá
my house is in a little harbour
in a queue for a Changó-bleeding flat bread
in the open sewers where extroverted rats live
and where rapacious mosquitoes fly
in a torrid theatre
the toy of erudite conquistadores
defeated by little blue princes and little dancing princesses

it is here where I am
it is here that I am not I
where silence obeys different rules
from 2:00 p.m. to 4:00 p.m.
and one dies
in the afternoon in Nuevitas
it is here where I would like to live
not to be a *real man*
not to be a *new man*
just to rest from all those years spent looking for you
to sleep without interrupted dreams
to listen to the sea knocking at the door

here is my house

THE ALPHABET OF THE TRAVELER

(2006)

PROLOGUE

to Luigi Mattiazzi

> There, all is order and beauty,
> Luxury calm and sensual pleasure.
> *(Invitation to a Journey)*
> Charles Baudelaire

The diaries of the traveler are like snowflakes. They are destined to melt. They are long and empty glances from the window of the train, of the airplane, from the bridge of the ship. They are the confirmations of spaces and solitudes; they are linguistic rehearsals, exercises to prolong boredom. The traveler we are talking about, doesn't count the seas, nor does he want to conquer the mountains. The traveler has weak arms and maybe he has a weak soul. He is certainly selfish but he is not bad. Harmless? Not always. The traveler is like a musician. He follows another music. His and nobody else's.

– TORONTO

ANONYMITY

The traveler is jealous of his anonymity, but the traveler cannot be anonymous. In many countries he has more money than the locals, in others he will be seen as a model of social displacement and therefore as an object of desire. The traveler is never called by name, sometimes people call him by the colour of his hair, or by the colour of his suit, or by the country where they think he is from (sic!). His name is brought to mind when he checks in at the hotel or when he shows his passport. If the traveler has a proper burial, (but the traveler wants to be cremated), that will be the only time that his name will stand still on this earth.

– TORONTO

BAG

The traveler needs a shoulder bag. Without a handle. His suitcase must have a handle. The traveler can also use a trunk. The trunk will be shipped from the last place the traveler stayed. A traveler doesn't carry a backpack. It is a demeaning tool for someone who is neither a boy scout, nor a mountain climber, nor an explorer. The traveler keeps the following items in the bag:

1 razor
shaving soap
toilette soap
shampoo
cologne
1 notebook (bigger than a moleskin)
1 sketchbook
1 box of charcoals and pencils
1 box of notepaper and envelopes
1 or 2 books
several pens

The traveler doesn't usually carry a camera.
He prefers to draw and mail the drawings to himself. As in the novel by Perec. The traveler is like a hermit crab. He carries his house on his shoulders.

— FROM THE BALCONY IN VIA ANGERA, MILANO

BOATS

Even the traveler smiles at the boats, and he smiles as well at the metaphors. The traveler uses the train, the ship, the airplane, as means of transportation. The traveler doesn't like to drive, he likes to be driven around. He chooses a place, but not the course. He is not a helmsman. A deviation doesn't bother him. The traveler doesn't follow any course.

– MONFALCONE

CLASSIC

It is during another stop that Egyptian statues are lined up for a transfer to the Arena. The traveler is consumed by the memory of the father who took his hand and brought him to the opera. It was respectful to dress up for the occasion, to wear the vest and the patent shoes too long and already too tight by the next opera. And the waiting, the bowtie, were becoming familiar like the caffelatte in the morning. But this is somebody else's past, not the traveler's. And the anguish is due to the missed chance. The Flavii reached their maximum splendor in the First Century D.C. So says the guide. The traveler doesn't see the guide, doesn't listen to the guide, because he is his own guide, not guiding himself. The traveler doesn't think about the family, about the consequences of the assumption to life, about the queues at the stores, about the original polyptic. The place is always new. The traveler doesn't go where he has already been. He doesn't go where a remembrance, a fresco, a flavor call him. The unknown, the unknowable, the unlearnable are benign gods of the traveler. His comet.

– VERONA, THE SANTA GIULIA

COMPLICITY

Was the traveler in the painting? Maybe the traveler was Attila? The traveler is not a murderer. He is the accessory to all murders because he has the nature of an accomplice. He looks and proceeds. Therefore he is not Attila. The traveler is not St. Orsola either. St. Orsola was traveling for a reason and the traveler has no objectives. Neither mundane, nor religious. Another personage in the painting is supposed to be Caravaggio. Was Caravaggio a traveler? Yes but he was mainly an artist. The traveler is not an artist. Maybe the traveler is the fourth person in the painting: the man who is trying to stop the arrow? If he did that he would have subverted his inner need to not be involved. The traveler is neutral but he also has feelings. He can be shocked by an event and for this reason the fourth character of the painting of the martyrdom of S. Orsola by Caravaggio could be a traveler, the traveler. The traveler goes through history trying to change its course. He changed throughout his itinerary to everywhere. His outstretched hand attests to the fact. There is no salvation. Life runs away. The traveler knows it. He has always known it.

– MILANO – PINACOTECA AMBROSIANA

FILM

A film is the closest thing to a journey; a film like a journey keeps rolling. But the film is always the same. The traveler is not fond of movies or photography. If the camera shot what the traveler sees without interruption, it could shoot until the death of the traveler. And where would a camera be placed? On the shoulders of the traveler? The traveler is not an archivist and memory is fallacious. Furthermore the traveler never stops traveling even when he dies. He has gone on some of the most beautiful journeys contemplating the ceiling, which is not a metaphor of transportation. Nor is it an allegory of transit.

– TORINO

GEOGRAPHY

Geography and anthropology. Religion, math, comics. And poetry.They are like flowers that the traveler picks in several corners of the earth, in coffee bars, at the post offices, in the railways stations, at the airports, in the temples, in the spaces, in the unspaces, in the emptiness. In the background of ceruse, in the philosophical wool, in the clouds.

– MILANO

HOTEL

Before his arrival the traveler dreams of lingering before opening the door of his room. The desk, the window, the bed and ah! the bathroom are the cardinal points, the corners of the world, the diminutive immanence. Only the traveler knows what fear and ecstasies match the sight of a writing desk which is shelter, barricade and bench in front of a window where he listens to the sound of the rain hitting the glass. He looks at the lightening of the merciless afternoon, which escapes the imperturbable venetians. And it is in front of the window which weakly reflects his curious eyes, his timid skin, that the traveler stops the time, awakens his memory, ordering it to bring him life and passions, lights and actions. Then full and drunk with reminiscences he lays on the bed and he starts a new trip to the meadow at the periphery of the city, to the dune, to the sea carpet... the traveler lies mute and stuffed with formulas of light and blood, silence and emptiness. Who is luckier than the traveler who doesn't know school, college or academy and to the fallen raises universal prayers, and whose world, rectangle or sphere, doesn't swallow into category?

– MILANO, BRESCIA, BERGAMO, TORINO, VERONA

JOURNEY

The traveler doesn't know why he travels. His passion could have started one morning many years ago when he went for a weekend in the country and he hated it. Father and mother woke him up early for fear of being caught in the traffic, and all the family was crammed in a small car for hours while his sisters sang endlessly on the road. Time was not his. So the journey for the traveler is an escape from his childhood memories. He believes that he cannot go against time so he lets time transport him.

— CUBA

LEAVES/SEASONS

When the traveler is able to avoid the passage of the seasons and to reach places where the leaves are still green, the traveler asks himself if he will ever die. Everybody can be infantile.

– HOLGUÍN

MOTHER

The mother of the traveler doesn't travel. She never traveled. She didn't like to travel. The traveler doesn't visit her often. The traveler must follow the journey and its rules. His mother knows and waits for a letter from him. Time passes and his mother dies. The traveler keeps writing her. In a strange city, with many celebrations and scarce humanity, the traveler receives a letter from the Mayor of his hometown stating that his mother has passed away. The traveler will never return to his hometown but he will borrow his mother eyes to see the shining falls and the whimsical sea and the sun peeping between the cracks of the palm leaves. The traveler will recognize his mother'shands in those of a librarian recommending a memoir of Gide's stay in Biskra. The traveler will warm up at the smile borrowed from his mother by a woman taking the bus. It is at sunset that the traveler hears her voice, carried by the waves, maybe by a summer breeze. It is during that hour that the traveler stops, it is during that hour that time stops, it is during that hour that he becomes the son again and he needs her.

— MILANO

POSTSCRIPT: THE END

The traveler is also a traveler of human beings and he crosses bodies and souls.

SOULS IN PLAIN CLOTHES

(2008)

THE GRAND TOUR

to Luigi, Carlo and Franca

It was not inside us
it was not outside of us
it was the union
a feeding of each other

in life we were destined to fail
our aim was to stay away
always
unable to participate in the grand tour of life
we drew imaginary maps in our heart
it was really eccentric!
Such places!
we fed ourselves with landscapes
and people
learning that there was life with or without us

had I been paper
you would have been the pen
and vice versa
and so on ad infinitum
through all the dialectics of the world
until we would have understood
that it was not the arrival at the port
that divided us
but the end of planning impossible travels together

OUR AFTERNOON BED

like many years ago mother
we laid on the bed
on the same bed
in the same afternoon light

you fell asleep before me
your wrinkled eyelids
sealed forever the perpetual dream
of renewing time
the distant whine of the windlass
the remote whistle of the motorcycle
the abrupt slam of the shutter
at times interrupted our nap

this neighborhood goes to bed in the afternoon
the sun pushes our souls into hiding
this is the bed where you were dying
after years of forecasting death
your heart was finally surrendering

some bodies our bodies!
some souls our souls!
you woke up and caressed my hands
I had forgotten the embrace
you whispered to me with words of a mother
and I did not know the words of a son anymore

CARLO

"respirare il padre" (Salvo)

soldier in three wars
desert survivor and p.o.w.
and businessman in your second life
you rejected the medal of honour
(I have always loved this story – less the motivations)
when you found your way back
you knocked at mother's door
with no hair, fake teeth and perforated eardrums
you were so emaciated that she didn't recognize you
but you needed no disguise to hide your defeated face
surely you had high hopes for your son
I withdrew from war by wandering in the streets
I was a prisoner of a sorceress for more than 12 years
surely I had high expectations for the two of you
no I didn't become a doctor or a lawyer and no
I didn't become a priest
my friends collected the papers I left in their homes
with some stumbling verses
perhaps I meant to pay for my board
or just to leave a trail of crumbs
I was not able to carry you on my shoulders
outside the city in flames
my little poems are on your grave
renegade words for the death of another unknown soldier

POEM OF THE MOTHER

has summer lingered with that vague stench of rubbish?
when the watermelon quenched you with a touch of sugar
is it still the summer of mirages of bucolic epiphanies?
of bicycles flying over the ditches?
of voices from the flock of birds far far away?
their whimsical syllables bouncing among the poplars?
not that you ever liked summer
you always praised spring
because summer lured reckless insects to the flowers of your dress
when those evenings whispered love
and you were listening to the disoriented animals
or were you confused by the sweat of your new body
before motherhood?
at last you could make shadows with the night lamp
in the nocturnal games with your sisters
laughing at your foolishness
the dead, if there's justice, are granted a return to youth
without work
without cry mama children
without husband
newly again new
who am I now? who am I for you?
do you remember when you were a child?
a question of a son who is not a son anymore
will you listen to my confession? could you again?
how many words will you hear?
and how much time has been given to you?
at last lucky you
time is no more
I mean the human time
original as the sin of living

THE MEMORY OF INDIA

It was not too long ago
or maybe it was a long time ago
but not enough to erase the memory
of a place where I have been
where the dream laid its body
where my hunger was terminated

In this place I felt my humanity
my strong and uncompromising flesh
I have never been to India
but I have memory of India

every tribunal in this land would condemn me
for pretending
I ask for the right to collect and treasure
the memories of places I have never been
of the man I have never been
of the dreams I have never had

LIKE ARTAUD USED TO SAY

to Sandro Martini

I knew that I could have died that morning
since awakening my chest was in a tumult
there was the serenity of a just and balanced fear
the certainty of my end
that sky and that wind of that dawn
last companions and witnesses of my departure

a flavour of execution
the hollow atmosphere of pain and of shame
I was a bit sorry anyway for the lack of hope
of transubstantiation
all things considered I said to myself
it doesn't even hurt
the air smelled of sea and freedom
and it could not be by chance

therefore I got dressed
choosing the proper clothes
with the humbleness and the diligence of someone who
wakes up every morning and goes to work
who stops at the newsstand to scrounge stories foreign to him
before taking the bus and scrounging passengers' familiar stories
I left the lunch on a chair in the kitchen
I left the bed religiously made

for I was going to be *suicided*
like Artaud used to say
for a death without a fire escape
for an end without a panic door

there was no fog and the light was turning on
among the ashes of a boreal night
in the park I waited trying to catch maternal messages
paternal invitations

friendly shouts
sounds of failure
victory whispers and secrets of hissing memory

I am simply passing away
cordially
I said to myself
tears were veiling my sight
though my dignity was sheltered
while time was imprisoned by this embrace
between nothing and nothingness
I am alive!

GRAZIE DEI FIORI

to Stefania

In me the residuals
of picnics in the Dolomites
gold and pepper and scented kisses and stone
strawberries
sisters singing
a good boy picking flowers
spring mother
oak father
yes love but fear a lot of fear
a sneaky son
dreaming of leaving forever
dreaming of coming back as a conqueror
sated and respected
the record skips
a new song from "*grazie dei fiori*" to
"*Coney Island baby*"
streets Christmas shelters
tasteless kisses
at war
diving into forgetfulness
have I been a bad son? no problem!
kisses flow again and words open their wings
mother is swallowed by pain
father is sailing to silence
sisters pick the last flowers
I compile a list of accomplishments:
two children
a woman
two orphan sisters
a full time job
some ambitions
several friends

I don't know why I am living here and
I wouldn't know where else I could live either
I write poetry
I can only hope that I will not outlive my kids
and that a thunderstorm will wash me away painlessly

FRUIT BASKET (CANESTRA DI FRUTTA)

(I met Caravaggio on a subway car)

This is only the beginning of a still life
there's death
                              and corruption
there's the magistry
                                        of life
and there's something more
                                                            the deceit
like the background of a wall
which stands witness
to death in motion
chipping and staining
the still life
incapable of stopping the course
                                                            of decay

FATHER

to Vanni , to Erio, and to M. Masud R. Khan

I can see
with your eyes
plains ending their race in the womb of mountains

restful seas like shadows of cobalt
in the corneas of the earth
things that you loved to watch
from the bridge of the ship

the sky giving birth at dawn
the half asleep snow drop

with your eyes
tears will not have weight anymore
my mind will walk to you
in a field laid fallow

I DON'T CARE ABOUT ANIMALS

to Deborah, Lou, Bella, Rufus, Rico

I have never been crazy about animals
I like horses, elephants and whales
I hate dogs, ideologically
I am not crazy about cats
though I like them ideologically
I have animals in my body
there is a hummingbird in my eyes
and one can feel the graze of his wings
no, I am not an angel
there's a hummingbird in my deeds
in my thoughts
you might notice it, see it, but
you cannot catch it
I love a dog, Spencer, because he is a great host
he introduces me to his friends
and he waits for my fortune cookie
we don't hunt together
we are just aging together
we listen to our approaching diseases
he is like a bartender
who listens to me
as part of his job
until we go home
on separate paths
my children are my pets
ideologically I sympathize with their love for me
they love me because I have a long nose and because
of my barrel chest and because
my prominent stomach is their playing field
but they are also forgetful when I am away
as long as there's somebody

their mother
my woman
she was with me in my previous lives
I was with her in her previous lives
her bones for me are the bones of the architecture
of shelter and abandonment
her jaws are banks seen from afar
I will tell you later about her shoulders and her calves
and her mouth which has the same energy of a sex athlete and a
renowned attorney
her eyes would force me to speak and write
and write and speak to audiences
there's a Mediterranean potion in them
yes there are waves but also the meadow and the stone
the olive tree and the cliff
the sky fallen into the sea
there's Icarus and Sisyphus
there's arrogance and punishment
there's chasteness and compassion
they quench their thirst at the
fountain of legend
she has the fragility of the prototype
and the gambling smile of the unconscious newcomer in the road

I stumble and mumble for your creation
as you stumble in my ranting
if I had real hands able to shape objects and fruit
you wouldn't be different
you have been a watermelon in the hottest
and blinding summer
you have been a grain of sand at the first convention
of the desert
the echo in the cave of prophecies, the prophecy itself

and a paintbrush, a note and, because you have your faults too, the
jaguar ambushing the toucan
have you been a wave?
the incarnation of a soul
embarking and stowing
the regret and the peace of departure?
before you I was asking for silence
being a stone fornicating with many millions
in the limbs of the Alps
under a vault of bodies
longing for the water or the rain
if I am a diamond for you
I also come from a crater
but I have been fast
so fast that no runner could dream of it
let me introduce myself
I have been a corpse in the rain
I have been an ant and a dictionary
of another language
I carry the fall, the ink and a strong stomach
I bring laziness and vanity
you carry the sight, the murmur, the trunk
and you bring inertia and capacity
we all had previous lives and the memory of them
keeps us unfinished
Andrea washes her teeth with the disdain and the disgust
of one plunging the bleeding sword in a river
Luca is testing the inexplicable teachings of growth
if they are animals it is because of their uncompromising ignorance

meet me at the oxymoron of peace
and of war
meet me at a safe distance
where and when my guilt rests

dawn ought to have your eyes
fog ought to have your smile
leaves ought to have your skin

I kneel in front of this world
which exists only for me
and I pray it remains mine

SOULS IN PLAIN CLOTHES

to Carlo, Andrea, Luca

Carlo,

on your behalf
I was searching
through the waters
of this peremptory injury
in the earth
and in an armistice between
life and death I wrote you
a poem, a letter
that you will never read
(though not everyone will agree)

I was sitting on a crust of a rock
among many people looking for whales
the tail, the flipper, the spurt

you would have spent hours breathing loudly
and praising the smell of this salty river
why are all these seekers here
stalking a miracle
to be healed
to be first to spot the whales?

the opposite bank is so far that
I feel I am still banned
from crossing
I am alive Carlo,
and I can see the whales with your eyes
and your name is on the waters
each wave carrying a name
the names of the dead
at last we see
a spraying wave

an effervescent soul knocking at our memory
are all the waves souls in disguise?
traveling souls in plain clothes?
waves in flesh and bones?

we all stand trying to recognize
our lost dear ones
all united and yet alone

Tadoussac
August 2006

THE LAKE IS OVER US

nomadic water pipes run underground
gentrified citizens assemble at the
ballots of unregistered grievances
somebody sees suddenly the vanished lake

there was a lake at the beginning of time
with gigantic trees

there was a time that you
could smell the lake weed early in the morning

buildings gated the community of
sirens and nymphs and gods

the impending skies
and the waters are only reflected
for the joy of a few
by the glass of the towers

the city thought it was closer to god
and over the city waves and boats were flying
it was easy for dreams to sail upward
it was easy for the rain to swell and fall

sometimes triggered by a crosswind
we feel the urgency of looking for water
when heaven parachutes a rainbow over the buildings

sometimes there are identifiable symptoms of alertness
when a passage appears through the greed of concrete
and our inexplicable thirst is quenched by the lake

by its mumbling waves
by the moored island
by the lure of distant lands

there's still a homeless person that remembers
the lake
and wants to run for mayor

EMBRACE THE WALLS

to Pier Giorgio Di Cicco

Over these roofs a muezzin could embrace the flames of sunset
in the radiant city so many democratic ears could vibrate with the sounds of diversity

the bells of the mass could orchestrate the flight of the seagulls
and too many could praise the urban legend of the global village
where neighbourhoods assemble to sing paeans to coexistence and tolerance

here they are: the ecstatic assembly of the endorsers
and the insatiable scavengers of ethnic food

the repetition of the whipping of the crucified man
the remake of the wreath of the conqueror
will make the neighbors feel at home

the walls set the time of nostalgia and displacement
the gates open to the mysticism of the old country
all these rivers of belief collect in a calm sea of righteousness
their streams itemized in hymns to government policies
boxed and packaged in a sea shell
that whispers the same word: pride pride pride

there's a juice in the flowers that only children
can drink
we are banned from bringing it to our lips
this is not what you would call prayer
this is not what you would call a miracle
and this is not because of original sin

champions of freedom and those who know the rationale
behind everything

advocates of multicultural transubstantiation
embrace the walls!

⁂

Can you hear a voice that lures us slowly to neutrality
and tolerance?
It's a refrain that reels off many warnings
and resembles the Pied Piper whose sounds
push us like mice into the invisible Lake Ontario
and we drown dragged down by concrete neologisms
Multiaccessmultiaddictmultiadvocatemultiarbitratormultiathlete
multiballotmultibarriomultibathroommultibombmulticavitymultiCa-
nadianmultichallengedmultichannelmulticitizenmulticleaning
multiclinicmulticoffeemulticondominiummulticulturalmulticunt
multidisciplinarymultidrugmultieducationmultiemailmultiemission-
multiethnicmultiexclusionmultiexhibitionmultiexitmultitextermi-
natormultifacemultifairmultifaithmultifinemultifuckmultinsuran-
cenumbermultigallerymultigarbagemultigendermultigentrification-
multiglobalmultiguidelinemultihomelessmultijailmultilandlordmul-
tinclusionmultintegrationmultilingualmultilovermultinativemulti-
mortgagemultineighbourhoodmultipersonalitymultiplanningmultipo-
etrymultipridemultiproductmultiracemultischlepmultisexmultishel-
termultisoldiermultitonguemultitolerantmultivictim
multivoicemail

⁂

Our city of backyards
of sanctuary of solitudes and familistic dreams
is plastered over with banners and posters of coexistence
gnawed by the rodents of tradition

souls hidden in basements
skyscraping souls in forgotten barrios

tenants are injected by city officials
steroids of rhetoric to fight
linguistic weaknesses and isolation illnesses

we are unfinished humans
in an unfinished city
where the wind blows the unleashed message
of opportunity and pride
pride in growing here
pride in loving this land
and despite the opposition of a municipal council
all this pride should be incinerated
for the most exhilarating emission
for the ultimate mass event
that will overcome the drums of Caribana
the shouts of Pride day
the laments of the procession
the assemblies of tribes
where the folkloristic gathering
mercilessly shows all our inabilities to pray alone

mother Toronto
embracing latitudes and parallels
and feeding us with limits and regulations
I strip you of your praised pride
I kill your ambassador
you are just a wide naked body
of blind residential serenity
and your crown of gold and diamond
is just a wall of condos
studded with plexiglass and concrete

it's your culture that spells
listen
it's your memory that moors
listen to the sea shell

if we all return to our
point of departure
this city would cry from Bay Street
to 905

embrace the walls!
these breasts of brick, concrete and metal
need your tears
embrace the walls!

what is civic aesthetic without vanity?
this proselytism of an urban gospel
of a global falling in love
with the city
is just coy voyeurism
at the orgies of high bohemians
could you fall in love with the veins of the metropolis
scarred by motors?
with the mute alleys of suburbs inhabited by
sleeping machines?

build a tower in Scarborough
erect a museum
put fashion in your window
confine the mayor over there
3 months a year
in distant Scarborough
and three months a year at Jane and Finch

mother Toronto it is time to evict art
time for the artists to expel paradigms
time for the artists to abandon museums
and galleries
if this is the place
we are the place
where we can bury
the metaphors under the snow
the snow of the Greater Tundra Area

embrace the walls
embrace the humility of the one who carries no history
the unknown citizen
doesn't need a monument
it is the artist that needs relocation

only the poet will not reuse reduce recycle
his words
only the poet will incinerate his soul
and poetry will finally reach the sky
embrace the walls!

NOSTALGIA

in Europe I could have injected
the ignorance of borders
or caged the sun
among relics of horizons
I could have died three times and
perjured and again traveled and flown
and stopped
here I close my eyes
they are biforas at night
in this impalpable organoleptic and north American suggestion

THE LEGEND OF DOWNLOADING

If I was there
I was unwittingly
training in the dogma of free choice
weaning from the supreme proletarian design

after forty days I came back with two truths
ignorance is a solid justification
misery was before poverty

then they downloaded me
into biodegradable files
and words faded
only the virus stood immortal

CINEMATIC TAXI

(2014)

HONEST ED'S

didn't you see them?   the races
sucking their teeth
spitting on subway platforms
throwing a hundred pounds of meat on the barbecue
buying tons of sugar
for fear of war
going into big stores
bait of voracious sects

dreaming of wardrobes with mirrored doors
buying bread and bread
stowing supermarket bags in the trunks of
american cars
buying gold and gold

sleeping in immigration offices
queued to go to unknown factories
in the suburbs of your sight
unloaded by a bus
on a Sunday

discounts
on leg of lamb
in line at the food-banks
in lines faint, drowsy, feverish

can't you see the fear of poverty
the steps of a second life
slippery from sweat?

sleeping little and always being sleepy
the brain wearied
from different languages

ONESTÉZ

Nun li vidisti i'razzi'e ?
sakiare i'dinti cu'ffischi de frontera
lanzando scaracchi su' banchi ov di sábuei
jettare e andred punti ov mit su'lbbarbecchiú
cumpra' tanzss ov sciugár
por scaggia de la ghera
ciargiari di cardz in da storo

rent the closezz co'i' anti uid mirrar
cumpra' pan y pan
fill co'nsupermarket beghe el maletéro
ov americancars
cumpra' gold & gold

durmi' in de immigrescion offis
in la láina ne' sabarbs de'a tu'ociada
jettati co'l paracadu' in annón factoris
lodati da un trocco
dominical

discaunz
en cuoscia de agneddu
in la láina alle fudbencs
in le láina smort, amodorradas, ca'fievre

e cu' non vitte a' paura ov poverti
di stepsss ov e second laiff'
scarlighent foar suét ?

durmi'...poco i siempre indurmentá'
lu' breinn straccu pe'
lingui d'atro monno

there are weddings
already marked by the violence of broken dreams

you so young
will lose your ethnic shape

will become fat and pakistani
you a varicose portuguese

your children will play be-se-ból
the turkish grandmother will watch football games on
television

you will build a fence around
your italian meatball
and put a sign on it
"please don't remind me of the past"

ci stan ueddíngs ia' marcade
da la viulensa ov brochen dríms

iu' so iang
t'impanzerai etnicamente

'daddiventare fat i paki
end iu' poltughiscc coi veni autdóar

i vostri cotrári plei a'beseból
a'madre turca taliera' u' futbóll
a la tiví

iu' bilderá''nafensa
araund iúr aitalian mitboll
cunt saina
"plias nun'me ricurda' u'passa'..."

MULTICULTURAL CHRISTMAS

the buildings in Comasina echo
from petit bourgeois christmases
to the roots of condominiums
kinetic junkies

in the spirals of housing projects
jamaican progeny
develop in darkness

italians clean fish
cries of a hundred babies
and neighborhoods in a frenzy

exhalations of incense
vomiting of curry and parked taxis
faint but strong-willed
a song makes its way
to my room

amore love amor
we are all immigrants
you are not excluded either
diaphanous jew
alone and without ideology
persecuted for a hundred years by the Bolsheviks

you will be there too cuban engineer
bonus in a tourist package
(walking one day with a flag)
toward the Skydome

no one is absent from the roll-call of races,
of origins, of creed
it is the christmas of the Charter of Rights

CRÍSMÁS MULTICRUTURÁL

di Comasina bildíng's risaund
ov Crísmás sufega'
ai rúzz de' bildíngs
tosici agita'

ne'irings de'iprojects
il midolo giameicán
crisci ne'ldarkk

di aitalians clín di fiscc
scríms ov andredz putei
i barrios in deliri

odúr de'ncensi
vomitade di cárri
chebs parcati end snorin'
legera ma sin scantu atraca una cansión
fin a'a mi rúm

amore amor ammuri
Uí ar óll immigranz
nianca tí te se'fora
sdilinquata Giú
sola i sin ideolohía
sgarrupata per undredz iears da'bolsevikk

Iú'll bi aiá ingegner cu-ána
bonus ov e tiuristic packegg
uán dei in camin
astal'ostadio

nisciuno falta a'laciamada de'razzi'e,
de'e origin,de'e confesión
lé 'lCrismás de'a Ciartovraitz trinca il vin matura' ne'ldarkk

disloyal Lolita toast to your
arrogance
fondled by suburban DJ's

you too are set in jewelry
... you too radiant princess
without jewels and without a land
infatuated with the last multicultural hybrid

and you that once
were a whore of the lebanese
and perhaps could confer upon yourself the title

of pearl of the West

today you have a son and a husband
from the third world
a Harvard graduate

a polyglot son
who does not take candies from strangers
and will die of aids

only because there are no more revolutions
you do not have to spend winters
in the bosom of your mother
you
will return
like all the thousands
the hundreds of thousands
of chinese, latin american,
from ex-nations
from ex-states

de cantin vecie (boccalun!)nevar fermenta' in di basamenti
tignusa Lolita trinca a'a tu''rogansa
filada daddigeis de'borgada

anca ti bela piedra per 'lgiuél
...anca ti bela prinsesa
sin giuéls i sin tiera
inamorada ov di last 'sperimentu multicrutural

i anca ti che taimm egó
l'eri 'aslandra de'libanés
i pereps te ciamavi

perla de'luestt

túdei ti te gá 'un puteo i 'un maridi
co'alaura
d'Árruard

n'figghiu che poliglotico
ciapa minga caremele da'lpedichiurr
i morera' sin duda ov éidzz

sol picché no'ncistannu mas rivolusión
ti te ghe no de migra'
tra'i zinne de'a madar
Ti
te vegnaré 'ndré
comm tutt 'itausandz
di undred tausandz
de' cines,sudamerican,
da ex cauntris
da'iexsteitt

maybe there will no longer be gigantic waves
inevitably
pulled by the undertow
onto these beaches

it is a snowstorm that is coming
we will learn

to show our most beautiful colours
multi-coloured balls
for the christmas tree

pereps no'saran mas i cavalún
sin duda
pusciati da'a risaca
ovar dis bicis

l'e' 'na tempesta de neff che ariva
Nu impareróm

a'displei auar most biútifúl colors
bale multicolorade
foar di crísmás trii

A TOAST TO ILLNESS

(2018)

MAGNA MORS

How can you be doubtful and let life lock the door
to freedom
Let death in
She is beautiful
standing there
with that dress no wife will ever wear
She has chosen you and you linger?

PROPERTY VALUE

to Deborah and Corrado

There are two of me
One has finished the painkillers,
the other one has authorization and access to a big stash
One is already planning a night of two or three movies
and nodding off between a philosopher's essay
and a letter from a relative
The other one
is a protagonist
of a film set in the Cold War

They are both approaching death
one with grey suits, regrets, and the other one with
the obsession of buying properties
We don't know when they'll both fall
The leaves in the backyard are still green and stalky
always a dead leaf
rebel bird killed by the out of season hunters
Watch out, the end of summer
watch out the sky
One oxycodone wouldn't hurt
it would help to close the deal

A TOAST TO ILLNESS

I am an old crippled monster
who looks asleep
when you are close to me
Don't talk don't move
and once I leave
dragging my big wrinkly tail
you can walk away
and stop at the first coffee bar
and drink
Don't move don't breathe
toast the old creature whose duty
is to kill and eat life beauty laughter!

SUICIDES

There are three suicides
the traditional one that gives you relief
the one that is imposed
and the one that is the homicide of the self

The third is the one that brings fear
because you keep toying with the idea
of the tool that will end your days

It is a mess to choose
A friend tells me that she had to put her two cats to sleep
One was resentful and belligerent
she was not cooperating
The other one fell asleep in her arms
after having cuddled gregariously

I'm confused, and I don't need a further option
Can I die when I don't know?
when I don't think?
Because this is what I have learned
there might be nobility in dying
in choosing death
but there is more deceit than anything else

We're forced to die
We're forced to put ourselves to sleep
Perhaps we'll have the privilege to not cooperate

BUT DEATH DOESN'T EAT, SHE ONLY DRINKS

Your question was straight
In fairness, you asked me if I could take it
Will you be here in twelve months?
Merda, merde, and so, mother ... shit
Is this a question to ask?

Yes I will be here
What is twelve?
Two halves of a year
Season + season = only six months
Snow, leaves, death
They will fall soon and I will do so
operatically, melancholically

I'll tell you what I'll do
I'll lock myself in the house
I'll wait for you
and I'll take some oxycodone
because I want to smile
if there will be fighting
Man versus cancer
And die, motherfucker

How will it be?
An impurity that forces me to watch the beyond
For somebody who has been in Paris
it was an epic end
Or I'll wait surrounded by relatives and friends
Some food will be offered
but death doesn't eat, she only drinks

In the month of August the stars were falling
and wishes were blossoming
Eight or nine months had passed

My achy body has not been able to sleep in a bed anymore
since December 12th, 2014
Then, it was that month's turn
They were falling like fruit flies
the wish still entrapped in their bodies

While months die, time goes past
and I ran out of Augusts
I was in bed, dreaming of Christmas
The Augusts were gone, and with them the stars
my wishes abandoned by the clouds

PREGNANT IN HABANA

I was in Habana feeding a squatter in my body
I was pregnant with cancer
That day that I went to visit the University of Arts
and when I bought those paintings from Monuelo
my stomach was bigger than his
His Orishas were in my fluids
I was still able to swim
like a fat triton in Varadero
to catch the ball over
the crest of the waves
I digested perfectly at the restaurant
and we walked in good spirits under the dark
and humid porches
until the rain fell
and we found shelter in a cab

I was drawing Habana on the bed in my bedroom
lying like a Roman
in the Habana Libre Hotel a bed 56 metres above the ground
watching the city, the sea, the Malecon
the furious clouds
the lightnings signalling the new borders
of the sky
This new life quantifiable in left-over days
hours of contemptuous ignorance
I was dying and I was dreaming about the future
the Habana, the Lymphoma
No city could better bear death sounding like an orchestra of
old and breathless musicians

It became a world of kindness
Everybody was so nice
Nobody could call you
hey you with cancer

and put a needle long as a sword
What has been given to me

This visa
This renewal of a permit with an unknown but sole
deadline
This ticket
What has been given to me
The torture of awareness of knowledge with no faith
The length of a candle
of a fuse to the dimmest
silent explosion that will not bring light to the earth

ANOTHER ROUND EMILIA

Poor little bird
Emilia taken by a melanoma
blown away like a cloud
I prayed for you
My pain weighs less than yours
I prayed with Lou Reed
I prayed with Leopoldo María Panero and Bill Evans
Some of us work with the laptop
We have a needle in our arm
Attached there is a machine like a pop distributor
The bell tolls vigorously and someone has finished the cycle of chemotherapy
I read that the word metastasis means movement, transposition
I am the mitosis spread from Italy to Canada
The oncologist tells me that my goal is to heal
One day I will end the cycle but I will not shake the bell
Because you could not
Emilia there is no reason to celebrate

THE POET AND THE CANCER

The oncologist increases my antibiotics and injections
So Rimbaud throws poems on the tables
Indications
Poetry is used in case of pernicious solitude
Counterindications
Do not take if your life is serene
Posology
One poem max 2 a day
to be taken after a meal
Collateral effects
cephalea, vertigo, anorexia diarrhea, alopecia
It contains
metaphora 30 mg, anomia, 10 mg, boredom 40 mg,

It gets expelled with the urine

XVI

I am a movie. A bad movie
which is not watched but watches the empty hall
I have seen a thousand movies

In these days and nights I have been seen by
a thousand movies

Of this winter I remember snowflakes and stills
a black and white blanket
without soundtrack

POEM OF ANIMALS AND OBJECTS

Thanks to Daniela Zanchi, Carlotta Beltrami, Allan Briesmaster

And to be afraid
the trembling animal with wet eyes
This is who I am
The gazelle that surrenders to the tusk
The mouse that waits for the dark
I close my eyes
I wait for the blade
Words and dreams
become prayer
The waiting
that dresses the silence

CHANGING RESIDENCE

*Thanks to Daniela Zanchi, Carlotta Beltrami,
Allan Briesmaster, Denis De Klerck*

I WAS BORN IN PARIS

to Franca

Dear,

The problem, if it is a problem, is that,
it is a bureaucratic oversight.
The oversight is that I was born in the wrong century.
I was born in 1854 in Paris.
I sleep in a hotel on the Left Bank out of laziness
and spend more than I have because money must circulate.
But who wants to waste hours dreaming of singing and writing?
I do! For this I respect the poor and all those who dream.
It is true that I generally do not like brute work
and eating and drinking for me are acts of freedom.
I realize that in Paris this mix of cultures and dreams
leads to walking in the park while people go to the factory,
to drinking in the square. When people eat dinner with their families
I sleep on a bench.
God, how useless I am! In the second last century,
in the last one and now. I am not productive
because my language doesn't include the word product.
I meet others like me during my travels
and I love exchanging words for hours and hours,
like Wilde in Biskra. I am waiting for you to come back
and in the meantime I am going to Africa, Asia and the Americas.
Only by ship and train. Rigorously. Why?
The train because it is like a moving womb.
The ship because the sound of the waves reinforces the dream.
The plane, oh my God, makes life dimmer.
And the airports—what an icy boredom!
We want to see the sky from below
because we are like ancient olive trees.
We have seen the history of human beings and their failures.
We are ready to tell this story and we always change the ending.

OUR DEAD

How much truth can a spirit bear
How much truth can a spirit dare? (Nietzsche)

Luckily, they died young before they surrendered,
before seeing the flesh age, before the varicose veins
scarred their calves, before the public got tired of their beauty.
Because beauty is boring and only captivating as the dose increases.
I can't help but think about the fallen heroes without saving any of
them.
I dedicate this poem to those who survived,
to those who sold their bodies and have no epigraphs,
to those who mocked the soul and at night crowd the cemeteries.
All of them floating in the poem of the sea.
A drowned man descends pensively, I am shipwrecked
in the sea of poetry .. Those who slept among the books,
who lived among books on which they placed coffee or a fried egg,
those who used to talk to books—can we live without them?
We can live without publishers. And without the poets who bartered
their written pages. Their body is gone. The body made of words
remains.
Immortal is the poet whose body never wears out.
I don't deserve to be called a poet, I don't deserve to be called an artist.
But you artists who died, leaving me painting canvases
that take every confidence, verses that reveal my most intimate
confessions—you didn't want me among you.
I fled then, seeking refuge in the guesthouses, in the cellars, in the
studios
of great professionals, leaving them at the dawn of their success
that came back like the light, while for me the night of anonymity
began at dawn. Can we live without them?
Terrible, says Orson Welles, the fake laughter on television.
The laughter of people who probably no longer exist and so
we listen to the laughter of the dead.
Are books, paintings or music, the noblest parts of the dead?

Their inheritance is truly the most important part of them.
The collections of porcelain, lead soldiers, dolls
are more important than their soul.

JUNKIES

When druggies get older
they have the eyes of good old people.
Life stopped one day
Philosophy, common sense, stopped at that cross light.
Who remembers the mean deeds one by one?
Junkies probably did some bad
but others did worse.
Junkies know.
They don't remember the bad, but they know
and they ask for forgiveness.
When they get older
their eyes show their repentance and their goodness,
even if they don't remember,
even if they don't want to remember.

BEFORE

everything had already been decided
that I had to die scared
taken care of
that I was not very smart
that my writing was that of a mentally ill person
and then gradually
I had to flee and when I returned among men
I had to display extreme feelings
the betrayal of that unjustified love
perennial Judas
in search of the most twisted tree
to offend my life
in that still monstrous landscape

COURAGE

to Ilario

Stay here where there is crying and gnashing of teeth
Where winter burns the lungs and I would not be able
to describe otherwise the pain that the cold inflicts on me
When my son doesn't say hello and he keeps playing
and his friends water down
this acid wine that is fatherly love with rebellious jokes
The son who laughs at you like
the male who asks and demands,
just as a prince enjoys the privilege
without affection
for a father who was not able to be a father
It takes courage, I say
To bear the gray, the leaden spread of ancient love.
It takes courage to work
money is the simple and eternal reason for being
and the fear of death and pain
accompanies the path without horizon
When prayer is a refutation of loss
And I'm alone
When poetry, colour and song
recede in the face of horror
Courage it takes
Courage that I don't have

SILENCE

to Claudia

Today we asked
that the rivers continue to feed us
may the undertow not stop drumming
let the seagulls fly through the storm in search of land

We are not ashamed to ask
indeed, we cry a spring rain
light rain
which at dawn is like steam,
breath of the trees
the whistle of birds

ITALIA

Certainly, my bones remember that thrill
that the Langhe helps you wear in the evening.
That sound of maritime pines' needles
Trampled by sandals
fill the silence that in the evening breaks with the diomedee*
The end of the race of the Mediterranean sun
and the birth of the evening creature
illuminate the sails and excite the demon

Finally
the echo of the wave wets the pale stucco of the island wall
the movement of the hanging garments inflated by the wind
invite you to leave the earth
among screams and the sound of the rowers
within the noble solitude of the mountains.
They tell me about my land
fight that stiffens time
I want you to know that I did not leave you alone
for your negligent motherhood
even if the detachment fills the nostrils and eyes and eardrums
here far from memories
Without you I would not know of life and death
of beginning and end.
The return to your arms will help me to surrender
because the return is the end of everything even if death is sweet

**Birds of the Tremiti islands.*

RAIN IN MILAN

to Stefania & Emilia

This morning in Milan
my sisters and I are getting ready
in a Situationist tumult.
Father is at home, and we go to the public gardens.
Mother says farewell at the door, and we think
that it is just right that she stays home to cook.
We take the number one streetcar and we approach
the gates of the city, of the riots,
of the public executions, and of the opera.
Emilia, Stefania, and I, take the picture on the pony
like frozen generals. We are at the zoo
and the elephant is shivering
and they push him out his musky cage
with a baton. The bear has a claustrophobic attack
We are happy. We come back home.
But before we buy the zuccotto at the best bakery.
Sunday ends with the results of soccer.
The bear is tired.
He will try to break the cage again.
He falls asleep under a rain
that falls over the cenotaphs and the canals
and the factories and the branches
with wild persimmons. Some are dead.
Father, mother, one sister,
the bear and the elephant.

Sunday in Toronto,
the music coming from the sky is the same
the old whale has sung
so somebody would remember
like I did

4 DIPINTI AL PRADO
LA CROCIFISSIONE/THE CRUCIFIXION (EL GRECO)

While the blood gushes
life sails from his body
the angel gathers the blood in his hand.
Don't let it fall.
It is a nurturing rain
and must not get muddied at his feet.
Christ's death is life for the men
but for the angel it is the horror
the rape of the son of God
by the hand of those who have no mercy.

Mary, Magdalene, and San Giovanni
from now on will be present in every painting.
That's the prize for their brave love

LA RESURREZIONE DEL SIGNORE / THE RESURRECTION OF THE LORD (EL GRECO)

Does Christ rise or fall?
His washed feet
still in the nail position
in confusion
in mirabilia the men gasp with fear
my Lord
I am on your left
I ask you with a nod to look at me
I would like to kiss your feet

LA PENTECOSTE/THE PENTECOST (EL GRECO)

These wise men might be self-righteous and boring.
They often talk about war and government.
They spent these great years with him
aging in the deserts and in refugee camps.
They are asked to bloom
they who fought an endless war.
They are like orphans
They are left alone with a woman
but this is the miracle
her lips open, maternal,
her singing gives them peace
and they welcome it

CRISTO IN PIETÀ E UN ANGELO/ THE DEAD CHRIST SUPPORTED BY AN ANGEL (ANTONELLO DA MESSINA)

That little swan wing of the angel seems too little
to support Christ
in the icy light
of the industrious and careless awakening.
The most terrible murder in history fills the canvas.
Dead is the Christ
the afflicted angel thinks
I finally cry because I cannot support your bruised body
but I do not sob
because you no longer suffer.
It is a song that comes out of
your loving lips.
Silence has won
even doubt

NIGHT IN CANADA

to Deborah

It rained love
and the flow of the humid night
gets stopped by the rustles of raccoons.
According to the numbers, tonight especially,
human beings unite and make love.
Perhaps at this time we will be able to love each other
sweating emerging flying
we will fall asleep
while the nocturnal animals hide.
I wish you understood
that the birds will sing today too.
It is Sunday.
For this you are happy.
Endless time without work
your whole body
seems like a journey with no return.

I WAS A BODY

to Franca

I was a naked body.
Curled into its blind and breathless exhaustion
I was everybody's flower,
sweat and nails in your flesh.
How do you want me?
Cockroach or leopard?

I asked do you want to stop here
in this house among the waves.
I can give you my hands
I was a naked body.
Curled into its blind and breathless exhaustion
I was everybody's flower,
sweat and nails in your flesh
and if you want me
how do you want me?
Cockroach or leopard?

I asked do you want to stop here
In this house lapped by the waves.
I can give you my hands.

Today a rotten chicken wing and a broken doll
share this couch.
You ended my life in Cuba
the afternoon that we found a shell.

Mother I wanted to be a diver.
You died before I could give you a pearl necklace.
My body is repentant and shy
before your words, your sighs.

I WAS NEVER TALL

to Rob

I was never tall
but today a flattened roof
the shingles blunt and chipped
the gloomy and filthy windows
covered by the breath of time...

So I am a hovel
almost abandoned
that the homeless avoid
because it is no longer a sanctuary for the living
but the haunt of ghosts

FOR YEARS

to Denis

I have not written for years
tarred and slow soul
for me the winds no longer blow
These stagnant and rotting waters
touch your walls
bystanders of the deaf and the dumb history
Many years have passed
that the ship has sailed
without the comfort of rest
I have not written any more

THE FALL

It will be autumn that appears
climbing the walls
where the flag of defeat
arches threateningly.
It will be autumn from the shy sun
malignant twin
of this gray spring afternoon
and one is the beginning and the other is the end.
Unable to accept the end of the end
when the leaf discolours as a faint note
and the wind ends like the song
of the boy singing at the end of the alley.
Here is the call
the last time
and we finally understand
its meaning

the fall
the dull and dumb look at the sky
autunno

WAITING LIST

I see a world that continues
flocks spread out in languid whispers
of branches in serene prayer
of churches that offer walls to the painter
of bread that smells of awakening
of olive trees that greet the boats
of mountains that know and teach
and vineyards that love and forgive
of bridges over the singing canals
of blue deserts and seas of sand
where I am a wave
a cloud
nameless
Will you recognize me?

A DWARF BUT NOT AVERAGE

With an operation
From one meter and 71 they shorten me to one meter and 54
Average height
From average height to mediocre
I become a dwarf
For years I complain
A monster is a monster
I'm a monster
Only today 9 September 2021
I am a happy dwarf
Not Poe's deformed dwarf
I am the deformed dwarf that everyone looks at and wants to own
Women wave their genitals in front of my nose
I am a dwarf and a dog that smells and whines
What does it take to be tall?
With those cloudy questions
Empty and dull
With that aerial happiness
that sea birds have
eyes close to the earth
you find pearls in the mud.
They were frozen tears today
butterflies fly in the sky
transparent lights
moaning stars.
The photograph of my face
is increasingly generous
whoever sees it feels the torment of the heart and
of intelligence.
The genius is low.
The genius is a dwarf?

TOMBSTONE

It was difficult
It was painful
But when the monster was ready
You were there
Mother and midwife

Art wants to be
courted by monsters

I am a monster
but I never loved art more than you

THE GREAT INVASION (WRITTEN IN COVID TIMES)

Like you locked up in a casket I will dress myself in light
That light that at night screams from a feverish reflection
on the distorted souls of human markets
My house is a convent.
I am St. Jerome
I got into the habit of writing sacred texts
During the day I pray in wisdom
and at night I reflect in the pallor of the waning moon.
Deaths loneliness poverty
"They are intolerable"
therefore, I write knowledge
My house is a convent
I am a monk awakened by knowledge
Survivor of invasion
Freed from darkness
One day the sun will illuminate these words
The flower will perfume your soul
In prayer I discover the game of creation
and the vicissitudes of the cross
Every day I see the world that will not be
God give me the life the hours and the time
Let me cover them with gold cloth.

PANDORA'S BOX

It came out after years of pushing in
I wasn't closing the lid
I was hurting my body and
I wanted to inform the world
That I was in pain
Only few were aware
I didn't need their compassion but their money

Then the box opened
And the ghosts were beautiful
Colourful and
some were singing
And they will sail me
To the quiet place of death

NOTES

PAGE 67, TONIGHT I AM THE STATE:

Libreta: Rationing card.

Hatuey: The Indian leader, Hatuey, tried to organize a rebellion against the Spanish in the 1530s. He was captured and burned alive.

Tropicana: The famous cabaret in Havana.

History will absolve me: After his capture in the attack on Moncada barracks in Santiago, Fidel Castro was put on trial. Castro defended himself. His defence speech is known to history by its concluding line, "History will absolve me."

Cristianos y Moros: National Cuban dish—rice and beans.

Balseros: People trying to flee Cuba by sailing on rafts.

Jineteras: Young Cuban prostitutes—the word may mean horse rider.

Periodo Especial: After the fall of the Soviet Union the Cuban government initiated a "Special Period" in 1990 of harsh new austerity measures and hardship to be borne by the large majority of Cubans.

Nuestra America: Title of a famous essay by José Martí.

Zafra: The harvest of the sugar cane.

Yemayá: The Goddess Orisha (Cuban syncretic cult—goddess of the Nigerian culture Yoruba—Santeria).

Changó/Shangó: The God Orisha, master of lightening.

The real man: The man described by José Martí in his essays. A new kind of figure embodying the Indian, the black and the white man.

The new man: The man idealized by Che Guevara.

LUCIO, YOU AND I

Lucio, you and I
have stolen the fire
we have freed the creation
that God wanted for himself
We caught the mane of the clouds
We have dressed the moon
and stripped naked the sun
that God wanted for himself
Only you and I
know the flame
vigilant sister
will lie close next to us
every sleepless night
and the morning flower moist with hope and dew
will once again teach love

poem published by SEF in 2022 in the collection
"un brindisi alla malattia "

LUCIO, TU ED IO

Lucio, tu ed io
abbiamo rubato il fuoco
svezzato il creato
che Dio voleva per se'.
abbiamo catturato la criniera delle nuvole
abbiamo vestito la luna
e spogliato il sole
che Dio voleva per se'.
Solo tu e io
sappiamo che la fiamma
vigile sorella
giacera' accanto a noi
In ogni notte insonne
e che il fiore del mattino, umido di rugiada e
di speranza
ancora una volta raccontera' l'amore

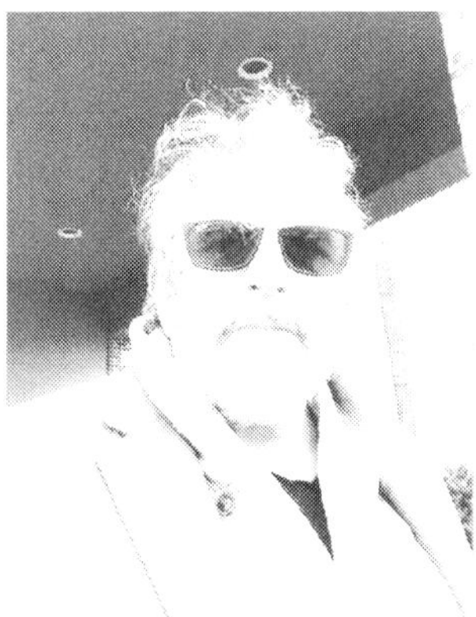

Corrado Paina lives and writes in Toronto. He was born in Milan, he dreams of living in Cuba, or in Venice, in Naples, in Matera, in Cosenza, and New York.